D1648547

READER BONUS!

Your investment in this book entitles you to a very special gift that is the foundation of *The Thriving Solopreneur*. It was because of this online training that this book was born.

It is a 7-part recording of an exclusive live training titled, **Your Critical 4 Hours a Week**, where attendees invested $226 to participate. And you can have it as my gift to you!

This training goes into greater detail on how to take the direct-mail features of your business, your online calendar and your address book to bring more people up-to-date with your latest offerings as a Solopreneur.

DOWNLOAD TODAY!

JanineBolon.com/readerbonus

THE
THRIVING
SOLOPRENEUR

Nurture Your Business
In Just 4 Hours a Week

JANINE BOLON

PRAISE FOR
THE THRIVING SOLOPRENEUR

"It was an easy read but packed with real life measures I feel I can immediately begin working on, downloading my contacts from various platforms into a .csv file. Who knew?"

Rebecca Rhea Collins
e-Merge Real Estate

"Wow! By page 15, I was ready to rush to implement what I have learned from this power-packed, jump start book. The simplicity of the processes to reach your warm market in order to foster bonding relationships is achievable. We can do this! Thank you, Janine, for your clear insight and guidance."

Michelle Mras
TedX Speaker & Keynote Speaking Coach

"Great book! I enjoyed it. Packed with great nuggets and to the point."

Darla Evon
Best-Selling Author & Speaker

"This book will inspire businesses that are just starting out as well as companies that have been in business for years. This process will keep every solopreneur focused on the strategy of working "ON" your business."

Lisa Ruef
Relationship Marketing Coach

"I found this to be a lovely, quick, and informative read! I've been dabbling a little side hustle and found the 4-hour principle to be very eye-opening! It actually answered several questions I've been asking myself about how to connect well with customers and continue to serve them, and it helped me to shift to a good service-oriented mindset of 'How can I best serve my customer?', rather than 'How can I make a lot of dollars?' That feels better to me."

Mindy Hardy
The Homeschooling Solopreneur

"Janine has created a blueprint for anyone to follow to be a success in any business. She not only gives you the concepts of business success but also the resources to implement to receive your desired results."

Gary Barnes
President, GaryBarnesInternational.com

ALSO BY JANINE BOLON

Money...It's Not Just for Rich People

Cash, Cars and College: A Young Person's Guide to Money Ditching Debt

The Grocery Store Game

10 Steps to Abundance

Seeking the Divine

Finding the Divine

Expressing the Divine (2021)

Cynthia —

Thank you for taking control of your own life and setting a plan in action for your success.

Wishing you much abundance,

James

October 2022

For Tina.

Published under the Copyright Laws of the Library of Congress of The United States of America, by:

The8Gates, LLC
1727 Main Street, #6386
Longmont, CO 80501-7311
720-684-6535

100520

CONTENTS

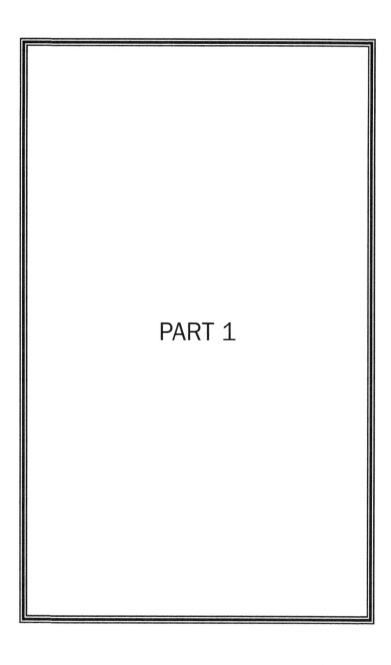

PART 1

WELCOME

WHO SHOULD READ
THIS BOOK?

Even though this book is designed to be read in about an hour, I don't want to waste your time if it's not a good fit.

Please take a few minutes and read this entire section to see if *The Thriving Solopreneur* is a smart investment of your time and focus. I wrote this quick read for three reasons:

1. To shift your focus from "working IN your business to working ON your business."

2. To share the 4 hours a week that I successfully use to grow and sustain my business.

3. To invite you to connect with me to determine if working together is our next step.

People in today's climate are seeking high-quality information to make smart decisions, save time and avoid mistakes. You and your product/service can do this for them. I want to help you expand your reach for your particular business while sustaining an organic growth in your customer base that will keep you in business for as long as you are enjoying working it.

I am unapologetically "selling" in this book, not only the concept of the Critical 4 Hours you need to be spending on your business each week but also why working directly with me to get your professional habits streamlined is a smart and effective shortcut to success and quick completion of your scheduling accountability.

If you're good with all this so far, allow me to further drill down into what type of business owner I've written this book for and who I know can benefit from the information inside.

I believe just about any business owner will profit from having these habits of the Critical 4 Hours working for them in their business, but there are four "types" who are ideal.

1. You're working full time and you have a side endeavor that you want to eventually move into a full-time business for yourself.

2. You're starting a business of your own and you know you don't want employees. Your plan is to remain a Solopreneur.

3. You've had a major life event occur (loss of job, parent/partner needs home care, etc.) that requires extra income on the side and you wish to build it in a few hours a week.

4. You're working full time and you've invested in a MLM (Arbonne, Mary Kay, doTerra, Young Living, Youngevity, etc.) and you really wish to grow your side business (MLM: Multi-Level Marketing Program).

These four types of business owners have unique needs to explain, clarify and position their products and/or services, which I believe are best served with a simple, easy-to-do system of working "on" their business in 4 hours a week.

Finally, *The Thriving Solopreneur* was written for the person who agrees with these seven beliefs:

1. Time is the most precious gift in our lives, and if we can connect and help others while taking up less time, we will be rewarded.

2. The written word containing useful information is one of the best ways to communicate why your products or services will help others solve a problem or take advantage of a new opportunity.

3. Sharing your personal story and stories of how you have helped others will uniquely humanize you and be the beginning of a

mutually beneficial relationship between you and your customers/clients.

4. You only have a moment to grab the interest of your targeted prospective customers amid the onslaught of competing marketing messages they are exposed to every day. Once you have their attention with your trial product or service example in their hands, you will have a more focused opportunity to communicate why they should invest in your product or service.

5. A real, professionally "constructed" printed card is one of the most powerful advantages and unique game changers in the business world for positioning you and attracting more ideal customers.

6. Direct mail is a welcome relief from bloated email inboxes, bills and circulars stuffed into our mailboxes, which contain unnecessary filler and are immediately relegated to the recycle bin.

7. A custom system of client acquisition is a business asset for you to create, and working with me is the key to getting it done fast and implemented pain-free in your own business cycle.

If you are like me and believe you can balance uplifting written content with making the case for you and your business and you are not afraid of making specific, "next step offers" for your readers to take, I wrote this book for you. So please keep reading.

MY PROMISE

I promise to make *The Thriving Solopreneur* a valuable use of your money, time and attention. Within the next 60 minutes or so, my intention is to open your eyes to the possibility and value of spending 4 hours a week on growing your business rather than working in the details of running your business. These protected 4 hours will be the fertile soil you've been looking for to attract, serve and keep more clients.

I will minimize the hype and bloat (found in a lot of business books), get right to the point and share the essentials of what you need to know as a business owner. Before we move on, I have two reminders for you. Regardless of whether you call the people you serve patients, students, or clients, for simplicity, I will refer to them as "prospects" or "customers" throughout the rest of this book.

Also, I am not going to spend much time trying to convince you that you need to spend these 4 hours a week on your business. A simple scan of the business marketing section of a bookstore will reveal many options to you on the importance of customer acquisition, retention and satisfaction.

I'm assuming if you are reading these words, you know the power of the systems and processes I teach business owners to grow their businesses using simple "goodwill" techniques with their prospects and customers.

Now to the magic of your critical 4 hours a week.

Your
Critical 4 Hours
are to
Your Business
what

Sunlight
&
Water
are to a
Thriving Garden

INTRODUCTION

S ince you're reading these words, I'm assuming you're OK with what I've shared so far and you are ready to join me for a rewarding 60 minutes as I share the magic of Your Critical 4 Hours to being a Thriving Solopreneur.

I have run my own businesses since I was 10 years old. My focus for business ran from selling products (my first franchise was Mary Kay) to creating an online university running 15 courses and coaching 441 students (The8Gates University). Last count, I have created, grown and sold over 14 businesses, and I started one nonprofit.

I was drawn to writing this book for you because of the interest generated in one of my online courses I was teaching. In this course, all of the students owned their own businesses or were involved in some sort of multi-level marketing program (MLMs like Arbonne, Mary Kay, Send Out Cards, doTerra, Young Living, Avon, etc.). They were so lost when it came to approaching prospects that I quickly realized most folks who wish to start their own businesses have no idea that there is a stepwise process to stay in business. This process is to attract customers, and once you have them, let them know you want to keep them around.

Keep them around? That's right. Over 68% of customers leave because they are not followed-up with. And they perceive that you, the business owner, don't care about keeping their business. Tragic, isn't it?

Many of my students had "zero" systems for prospect management, follow-up and business training for their team. So much of my life experience was just that. I was trained as an analytical biochemist, and I worked in the pharmaceutical industry for over a decade in automation and robotics. It was my job to streamline processes and to simplify drug-development systems as we moved compounds through the gauntlet of scientific inquiry to the patient.

No matter what my full-time job was, I always had a side endeavor that kept my creative side alive and well. For me, business is fun. It is a way for me to fully express myself, my ideas and not have to deal with any restrictions on my creative process. That is why profitability is so important to me. I know that what I have to offer my community of customers is going to make their lives easier, simpler and calmer. The higher my profit margin, the more services and products I can offer my community to improve their lives. Everyone wins, and that makes me super happy.

Enjoy your critical 4 hours a week that keeps your creativity inspired, your community aware of your talents and your pocketbook operating in a positive cash flow. We want you to stay in business so that you can keep serving your community with the excellent products and services you've created that make their lives better, calmer and full of beauty.

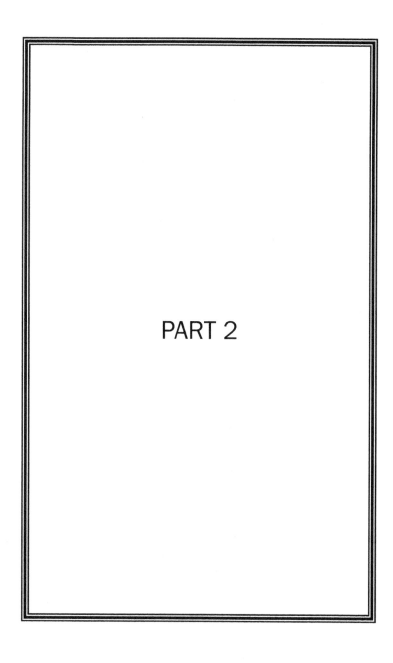

PART 2

THE 4 HOURS A WEEK BLUEPRINT

Prospecting
Follow-Up
Connecting
Training

CHAPTER 1

YOUR CRITICAL
4 HOURS A WEEK

I started my first service business by taking out a loan. I borrowed $39 from my mom to have t-shirts and hats made with my logo screen printed on them. I had just created J-Bon's Helping Hands, a domestic and professional cleaning service, and had partnered with my sister.

We were working for $8 an hour for people, and we'd split the money in half after each job. I remember that was the hardest money I ever worked for in my life and made a promise to myself that I would never again take out a loan to start a business.

Fast forward 10 years and I found myself borrowing money against an old truck I owned. I needed some seed money for inventory for my Mary Kay business, and with $1,000 from the bank, I had enough product to get rolling with customers. That loan was paid off in a few months, and I was given a lifetime of training from the systems Mary Kay Ash used to train her consultants. I will be forever grateful for the training programs, the upline leadership I had and the work I put into helping women look and feel better about themselves through self-employment.

It was through these businesses and 12 others that I learned how important systems are to your sustainability in business. Business owners are highly creative problem solvers and artists, although they may not see themselves that way. Many Solopreneurs flat out told me they weren't artists, but when I saw the problems they were solving, I had to disagree.

They were amazingly talented, gifted people, and it was because of their mental gifts and physical adaptability that they needed to work at a side gig. Why? Because working a full-time job keeps food on the table but is not enough to keep their minds engaged.

As a Solopreneur, we wear many different hats as we run our business. It is important that you pay special attention to your calendar when you're setting up your week. Remember that old adage: "Know the difference between working IN your business and working ON your business"? As a young business owner, I heard that statement a lot from the top salespeople of the day, such as Brian Tracy, Earl

Nightingale, and Lloyd Conant. As I tried to decipher what this meant, it would take me seven years to understand the difference, and it would revolutionize the way I thought about my business and the way I would run it.

These Critical 4 Hours that I am sharing with you are the core of working ON your business. This time that you spend each week on your business is what keeps you profitable and keeps a steady stream of new prospects, clients and customers walking through your doors or messaging you on your phone. It is the organic way to build a business, and it allows you to continue to live a high quality of life without your business consuming your every waking hour. Isn't that why we got into business in the first place? Because we wanted a different life than the one that was presented to us? I hear you saying YES! So let's get on to the Critical 4 Hours required to keep your business in a slow but steady growth phase.

CHAPTER 2

PROSPECTING

Prospecting is all about one thing: building rapport with people you want to get to know better. Creating connection with people is one of the largest misunderstandings I have ever seen in the business world.

This is not about selling.

This is not about getting people to a point where you can tell them all about yourself.

Prospecting is about learning the needs, wants and circumstances of the people you are coming into contact with. Many of us got our start in self-employment based on a customer or project. Either that, or we had a product or idea that we thought would be of great benefit to those around us. Whatever the initial reason for your foray into the world of

Solopreneurship, the point is that you will need to fertilize your customer base from time to time.

When do you do this? The perfect time to start looking for new customers is now. It doesn't matter when you read this book or when you started your business. Look for customers now. And when you meet them, be extremely selective about who you spend your time with.

Before I ever start looking for a client, I look for people that I want to work with, which are folks who are easy to get along with and who I enjoy having a conversation with. Yes, I'm very picky! Why? Because I know that my business services are for very specific people. They must meet a set of criteria, or we don't work together. Just like planting a garden, you don't just throw seeds on the soil and expect them to produce bounty.

When I first started working in the Solopreneur world, I made sure that each person I spoke with never felt like they were my "target" or a "prospect." I never directly "sold" to them. I want people to feel at ease with me so that I can learn as much as I can about their lives, their needs and how I can support them as a fellow business owner or as a member of their community.

The point of Prospecting one hour a week is to make contact with and gather information about as many new people as you can before you move into your next stage of follow-up. This is about getting to know people as people, first. You want to create a large lake of folks who you can contact about your latest news, products and services. This group falls into the category of contacts. Answer this question for me: "*How many people do you know?*"

There are three primary places to go for this information:

1. Your current clients
2. Your phone
3. Your social media

Let's break down the list of folks in your world already.

Your Current Clients

If you've just started a business you may have only one or two people who are paying clients. That's fine, even if you are at zero clients, you're still okay with this system.

The folks that have already bought into your business are gold. These are folks that I continually stay in contact with by sending them cards that are just little reminders that I appreciate them doing business with me. We will discuss this group of contacts more in the Follow-Up section.

Your Phone

These are the people I already know and have started a relationship with of some kind. These are people I like and folks who I do not want to alienate with my business. I want them to know that my business is here as a service to them in building a better community. I want them to see me as a team player for their life.

Here is where I will contact everyone in my phone using a system that has me list them in a database file where I keep my notes and suggestions for future contact. Did you know that you can access the contacts in your phone and print off the entire list as a .csv file? I recommend that you do that right now. If you have Google contacts, even better.

Create your prospect list from your phone, and realize that these people are who you will be contacting for referrals. You will NOT sell to them. It is important, however, that this group of people be in close understanding about what you do. This is the list of folks that will get you your warm leads, referrals and introduce you to the new people that will assist you in getting you the clients who you can best serve and help.

Remember to reach out to your vendors, suppliers and consultants about what you do. They are incredibly important to your referral system. If you don't know how to download a .csv file or you don't know what I'm talking about, I have a video that explains all this here: **JanineBolon.com/csv**.

Your Social Media

How many people are you connected with on LinkedIn? How many people are you connected with on Facebook? Instagram? Twitter? Alignable?

All of these social media platforms are great places to get to know more people and see if they qualify to be a lead, referral or someone who can guide you to the groups of people who you can best serve.

For me, when I first started using this process, I decided that my form of prospecting would be obtaining the addresses of everyone that made connections with me on various social media platforms. I decided to send a card to the people I knew. It was time to show people I cared about them through the mail by sending them cards.

People loved receiving my "good mail" in their mailbox. My cards are personalized and spoke to them as human beings on planet Earth. As my dear friend, Susan of DoodleMama Design, said to me, "*Janine, this is Good Mail.*" Hence, she coined the phrase I now use on a daily basis.

This is what I do to build my Prospecting Base:

- I learned how to download .csv files of all the contacts on my phone, Facebook Friends and LinkedIn Connections (free videos here: **JanineBolon.com/csv**).

- I built one huge .csv file that had everyone I was connected to listed (you can use Google-Sheets, Excel, or Numbers for this activity).

- I deleted extraneous data that I didn't want from the .csv.

- I called, texted or messaged as many people as I could in an hour asking them for their address because I wanted to send them a card (i.e., "Good Mail").

- I put a check mark next to each person I reached out to.

- I did this for an hour every week.

As of this writing, I still haven't gotten through the 4,228 contacts I downloaded from my initial phone, Facebook and Linkedin connections in 2017. More contacts keep being added every day! Right? The point is you are continually reaching out to new people every week that are warm leads. These people already have connected with you in some way, and no matter how tenuous the connection is on social media, it is still a connection.

Gone are the days of cold calling. Today all you have to do is pick up the phone and start calling people that you already know. Don't know what to say? Then give me a call and ask for some training. Or visit my website and sign up for my Tele-phoneTalk class where I share with you recordings of the conversations between prospects and me as well as easy-to-follow scripts for your beginning phone conversations.

Follow-Up

CHAPTER 3

FOLLOW-UP

Over and over again, I have heard it said that "The Fortune is in the Follow-Up," and this is quite true. I have proved it to myself over the past 40 years, and I've been tagged as the "Queen of Follow-Up" by several of my strategic partners.

Many people in our world are running at a speed-of-light pace, and they need the opportunity to be reminded of who you are and what you are able to do for them through your product or service.

We hear this mention of "Follow-Up," and yet that is where most Solopreneurs break down in their sales cycle with prospects, customers and vendors. They don't have a system in place for all the business cards, contacts, connections or people they meet on a daily basis.

Do people know what you do?

Do they know how you can help them?

Sharing with them only once is not enough. But continual reminders of what you do is helpful, and you can do it without selling, without hassling, without pitching.

One of my favorite images for the sales cycle comes from Josh Turner (https://connect365.io/), in his Connect365 presentation (used with his permission). In it, he mentions the importance of Follow-Up with this revealing graphic:

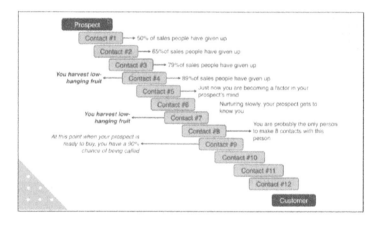

I took one look at this cycle and knew that I was going to have to create a novel system for myself in order to keep my business humming along.

How could I do this without selling, without being a pain, without being pushy?

That is when I hit upon the one thing I love doing. Sending letters. However, to sit and do follow-up for my people by sending letters was way too much of a challenge. I decided that I would send short, quick notes on personalized stationary. I was sending 10–15 cards a day doing this, and it was taking me several hours, not to mention the added time of addressing envelopes, stamping the envelopes and post office runs.

It didn't take me long to realize I needed a better system. At this point, I started looking at the various direct mail businesses and quickly realized none of them could customize the cards in the way I needed. I wanted to send cards that really connected with my people. I didn't want my cards to look like they were a system. I wanted my cards to be a reflection of me, goofy humor and all.

It was then that I ran into an MLM firm called SendOutCards. I had no desire to create "another" business, so I became a customer and came up with a systemized way of sending not only personalized "heart-felt" cards but I also used their system to send batches of cards when I had online courses to promote or I was offering a presale coupon on a new book I had written. SendOutCards prints, addresses and stamps the cards for me. I customize them on my desktop or use the app on my phone, hit the send button and the rest is done for me.

This system of sending cards and using direct-mail techniques is the single best goodwill effort I have ever used. It was through this system that I realized I had a 98.4% open rate on my cards (the other 1.6% get returned from the post office). If somebody moves, I know about it within a few weeks. If a house is sold or there is a job transfer, I'm usually one of the first people to find out because of the change of address.

This is a huge boon for me and my business. In my email campaigns and my online efforts, I have to expend 2–3 times as much money and the same amount of time to get 0.8%–2.4% open rates.

By the end of April 2020, I knew that people's email inboxes were being swamped out by the global conversion to online business due to COVID-19. I slowed my email marketing to the bare minimum of a monthly newsletter and focused 95% of my efforts on direct mailing of my promotional materials. It worked.

This is what I did to ramp up my business during one of the largest global shutdowns in modern history. Below is the exact system I used to grow my business after losing $28,000 in speaking fees due to the pandemic.

1. Go to your Facebook account and download every "friend" you have into a .csv file (Excel

    Spreadsheet or other preferred format).

2. Go to your LinkedIn account and download every "connection" you have into the same .csv spreadsheet.

3. Go to your phone and download every "contact" you have into the same spreadsheet.

4. After you have all the names listed of everyone you know, start sending people cards. If you don't have their address, call, text, Facebook Message and get their preferred mailing address.

5. When Facebook tells you that a "friend" of yours is having a birthday and you don't have their mailing address, sing "Happy Birthday" using voice messaging, and ask them to send you their address so you can follow up with a card.

This was all I did in my marketing and prospecting for 90 days, and I grew my business from 286 contacts with addresses to 433 contacts with addresses. These are warm leads.

The difference of me reaching out to a warm lead or a cold lead is astronomical. Warm leads have connected with me. In the Facebook and LinkedIn worlds, these prospects have reached out to me to ask me what I do. They have wanted me in their life. With that in mind, when their birthday comes up, I send them a card along with a song. Do I sing well? No! Do I sing with laughter, joy and fun? Yes! That makes all the difference. I have taken a moment to brighten their day, and I'm offering to send them a card later. No one minded that they were going to be receiving a birthday card after their birthday. Most were thrilled that I offered to send them "Good Mail."

Now, not all of the folks that I sang "Happy Birthday" to would send me their address, but all of them gave me a response of some kind, such as a thumbs up, a "thank you," etc. I never had this much response from any of my other forms of marketing that I had paid thousands of dollars to implement or hours of my time in the training. These other systems were inefficient use of my time and efforts. Such is the life of a Solopreneur. Our systems require different forms of communication and contact.

The easiest form of follow-up is the one that allows you to be you: completely, authentically, unashamedly. This also lets your prospect know you care about them and that you wish to make their life better with the product or service that you are offering. Mailing cards makes it easy for me to stay top of mind. I use the back cover of my cards as "advertising" space with a very heartfelt, personal message on the inside.

If you wish to learn more about the uses and benefits of Follow-Up, watch the videos in your Reader Bonus where I describe this in detail. (**JanineBolon.com/readerbonus**).

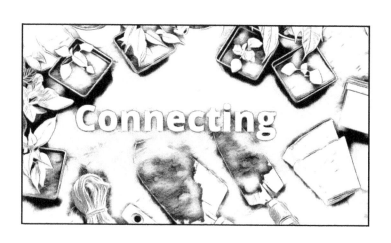
Connecting

CHAPTER 4

CONNECTING

You may have seen this section of "Connecting" called Closing. "Always be closing" used to be a constant refrain. Basically, in the sales world, this was the attitude and affirmation used every minute of every day by salespeople for any product they were trying to get a customer to buy.

"Always be closing" is a mindset that demands from the seller that you are to use whatever tactics are necessary short of out-and-out lying to get your product into the hands of your customer. They trade price for time and have horrendous time constraints and quarterly quotas to meet. The pressure on this type of business is awful and has nothing to do with what you are accomplishing in this modern time.

This sort of sales technique is a dinosaur in today's service-based economy and social media environment.

You will fail, and fail BIG, with this technique as a Solopreneur.

We are service-based people. We are heart-based people. We are the servant leaders that are talked about in the media. If we do sell a product, it is to make the world a better place or to serve the needs of our customers and our communities. The relationship between producer and customer has never been more transparent or quick, thanks to the internet and social media.

Farmers can now do Facebook Live from their tractors as they discuss the next crop going into the fields and how their organic growing processes are best with their crop rotation techniques. Seamstresses can share with you techniques on how to tailor an outfit that they have made for you. And if your dryer stops drying but continues to spin, you can go onto YouTube and learn how to fix it yourself. (True story. Happened to me last year.)

These contacts with customers are not at all the same as the sales tactics used for decades to promote products and manufactured goods. In our new service-based economy, with intellectual property and consulting services, this particular business strategy must transform from Closing into Connecting.

Connection is what makes business personal and has brought about the term "Relationship Marketing." If you are a Solopreneur that sells your knowledge base, intellectual property or consulting services, you are required to be in Relationship Marketing. If you wish to allow your business to blossom and grow, then get to work building relationships while you build your business. With this new shift in mindset, our mantra is all about "Always be listening!" Listen to what your prospects and customers are saying about themselves and what they are experiencing in their lives.

Most of my sales from the relationships I nurture happen AFTER 90 days. You're probably wondering, "After 90 days from what?" Many of my sales occur 90 days after my first presentation that I shared with a prospect (or a ZOOM room full of people) about what I do. It is important that you have a system of follow-up and continually connect with your prospects for 90 days (or more) so that you keep your customer pipeline moving in a positive direction.

Connection requires only a single action.

Commitment.

Commit right now that you will return to every prospect that you give a presentation to. This requires at least an hour a week where you are going back to the folks you've presented to and letting them know exactly what you remember from your previous conversation and asking them how they are, what's new in their world and what you can do to make their lives easier. Guess what you do then? Stop talking. Listen. Take notes.

This is the atmosphere in the marketing world that is proving to be the primary income-generating tactic. It is this process that allows Solopreneurs to carve out specific times and dates to return to their prospects. They can follow up with their clients a second and a third time to request yet another opportunity to chat with them. In the Connection stage of building a business, your primary goal is simple. Right before you hang up with someone or are about ready to wrap up an online presentation, make sure you schedule the next appointment with them. Ask for the next meeting.

In my system of follow-up, I sing "Happy Birthday" to people. During my stage of connection, I'll be asking them to get on a phone call or Zoom meeting with me. I even have a special page on my website for people to schedule time with me.

The Connection Hour of your week is you going through all the people you've given presentations to, folks who had you on their podcast show, folks who have referred people to you, etc. This is where you build your business by returning to people who you've already spoken to three times or more. And when they pick up the phone or you message them on LinkedIn, you ask, *"Hey, Linda, how's business treating you?"* or *"Are you doing okay, Mike; how's the new project?"*

By leaving phone messages or voice messages on social media, your people will hear your voice and hear the care and concern you have for them. Over the past year, I have left hundreds of voice messages on Facebook Messenger to my contacts who have had major life events happen to them. Sometimes we just don't know what to say to someone to help them through a tough time. Guess what? That's what I say in my Facebook message to them:

"Hi, Tracy, I see from your Facebook post yesterday that our mutual friend, Lisa, passed away. I have no idea what to say right now. I really don't, other than, I'm sorry for your loss."

And I leave it at that.

Sometimes I see a celebration or an accomplishment that a person has experienced. They've graduated with a degree, they finished dental hygienist training or a new certification program. I leave voice messages of congratulations and ask them, *"Hey, Sara, let's hop on a zoom meeting, and I'd love for you to tell me what inspired you to go after that certification in the first place? I don't know that story, and I'd love to hear it."*

It is this sort of conversation that will keep you top of mind with folks as well as guide you on what is happening in your community of people. I have received most of my speaking opportunities from folks who started off chatting about what was going on in their lives, the groups they are a part of and the value of the information they thought I could bring to their people.

I know as a Solopreneur you already know this, but I'm going to risk repeating it to you. As much as you need to make a living with the product or service you provide, your people need to know they can trust you with their hard-earned money. By taking an hour a week to call folks and celebrate with them, listen to them and connect with them with absolutely no intention of "selling" to them, your trust factor will go through the roof in their minds.

It is imperative that when you first start talking to people that you spend the first connection with them talking about them. If they ask you what you do, don't tell them. Turn the tables and say, *"Thanks for asking, Kyle, but I really called to find out more about what's going on with your business and how your latest coaching program is going. I'll be happy to talk about me in a minute. So tell me about this new product you're offering people."*

Then listen. Take notes. Ask questions.

This is an old technique called conversation. The art of conversation on the phone, in "live" online meetings and in person is a skill that is cultivated and must be practiced. No one is born with the gift of conversation. Some folks are more extroverted than others, but even some of the most introverted people I know have a skill for conversation that is full of depth and intimacy rather than sounding flat.

Spend time writing out a list of questions you'd like to know about a person. Even if you are speaking to a person that you know really well, there is always more to learn. People change. Thoughts change. Experiences change for your people. Ask them about their dreams, goals, what's new. The list is quite endless.

The biggest point in the Connection phase is this: relax! Ask them to talk about themselves, and if you are in conversation #2 or #3 with them, then tell them what you do, but make it something you can say in a single sentence. I would prefer you be able to tell them what you do in five words. When people ask me what I do, I say, "*Oh, I'm a Financial First Responder.*"

The response is usually silence, which is good. They're thinking if they have any clue what that is. Most ask, "*What is that exactly?*"

"I guide people from where they are financially into greater abundance. If they're in debt, they will become debt-free with my systems. If they're saving for a house, we get them there; you know stuff like that."

Then I drop it. I don't tell them about my 15 online courses. I don't tell them about my 4 podcast shows. I don't mention any of that. I go back to my connection and say, *"How are you doing with your current schooling/job/hobby, etc.?"*

The point is you are connecting with people. You're building a relationship, and you can't do that if you're talking to them with an agenda in your head about what you're going to "sell" them today. Your job is to be present in the moment. You should be thinking about how you can be of service to this person's current needs, and you can't hear what they are saying about that if you're busy thinking about how to sell them your product or program.

Your goal with every phone call or zoom meeting is that you have the next call or meeting scheduled before you end the first one.

Now, you may be thinking that all this connecting takes time. Yes, it does, but your prospect's business is worth it, isn't it? You are investing in your community before they invest in you. I've had people ask me to speak in front of their groups because they got so uncomfortable with the amount of service I gave them without asking for anything in return. These speaking gigs allowed me to be in the front of 25–85 new faces. It is amazing opportunities like this that come about because you are willing to invest in your connections, first.

Here are the primary points of your Connection Hour you do each week.

Before you pick up the phone to call someone, be sure to:

1. Have a list of questions to ask them. You have chatted with them twice before, and you have notes from your conversations (Remember that massive spreadsheet?). It is good to list out some additional questions for them

2. Have areas that you think your business service or product can help them with their time, money or health.

3. Be "present" on the call/meeting. This means that the entire focus is on the other person. Don't phase out while they are speaking. If you don't understand what I mean by "active listening," go onto YouTube and watch a few presentations or TedTalks on how to listen. Seriously, it is that important to your bottom line as a businessperson.

4. Smile. Smile while you're speaking to your connection or leaving a message. A smile will travel across the miles. Seriously! When I was 18 years old and working for a highly gifted woman who marketed banking services to Fortune 100 companies, she trained me to call on her customers and ask for appointments. On my first day at the desk, she planted a mirror next to the business phone and instructed me to look at myself before I ever picked up the ringing telephone. Upon lifting the receiver to my face, I was to smile and say, "Hi, you have reached [Business Name]. This is Janine. How are you today?"

If you feel your phone skills are a bit rusty and you'd like some practice, hop on a call with me and we can decide on the best plan of action for you. Visit **JanineBolon.com/talk** to schedule.

Smile!

You're Gorgeous
when
You Smile!

Besides, it is a
mood elevator
and we can all
enjoy
being in a
great mood.

CHAPTER 5

TRAINING

This is your crucial next step, personally and professionally. Take an hour a week and start training yourself. For me, this means that I read books on marketing, systems management, personal processes and financial development. I learn the new software upgrades, or I take that hour to read over articles in the latest Financial Management blog or Relationship Marketing magazine. The point is to keep yourself fresh. It is important to keep in touch with the trends and resources available to you and your customers in your industry.

Why?

Because this is how you can charge as much as you do. You are a professional in your industry. You are one of the few that can adapt and change quickly when the economy shakes and quakes. You have the ability to adapt in ways larger groups and organizations cannot. Part of your assets is your ability to take the time to read, digest and implement fresh strategies that others are too busy working "in" their business to make the time to work "on" their business.

Some suggestions for training yourself:

1. Read a book in your industry.
2. Read a group of articles you've bookmarked from previous days.
3. Listen to a podcast in your industry.
4. Take notes from a recorded webinar you were unable to attend.
5. Look over those old conference notes that you took years before, and see if any of your epiphanies you scribbled in your notes back then are appropriate for your business now.
6. Take an online course that will improve an area you wish to strengthen.

All of these activities are making the case for your own self-improvement and knowledge base. This is strategic and critical for you to remain finely tuned to your business, industry and customers. Being a Solopreneur is really a journey of self-discovery with the opportunity for self-improvement along your journey to profitability. If you don't like learning new things, if you don't like having to create new plans, strategies or systems, then it is time for you to re-think your current career path as a Solopreneur.

As a Solopreneur's knowledge base, skill sets and experience grows, so should your income. If you've been doing the same sort of work for over 15 years, you should be paid as the master level of your craft, right? How do you go about setting your pricing structure and marketing your unique brand of business? Those questions are beyond the scope of this book, but that is why it is important that you spend an hour a week working on your personal training in business. You always have more to learn. There is always another skill, certification or program that you can take that will allow you to charge more for your services.

Take the time to add value to yourself and your community by building your skills in the areas that you find exciting and fun to do. It is important that you make enough money so that you can contract out the work that you don't want to do so that you can spend more time working on the areas of your business that you adore. Those areas of business that you enjoy most are the passion pieces of your work that thrill you each time you step up to engage in them.

Remember, as the business owner, you are the only one that carries around the vision of what you want your company to do, be and have. You are the only person that has full, intimate knowledge of the mental image of vision in your head that is the initial dream that brought your business into this three-dimensional world.

Each of us has a unique set of skills and dynamic perspective on how we view problems. And more importantly, we have the solutions we create to assist others. Keep your brain perky by giving it new information that builds your strengths and guides us (your customers and associates) around life in gentle ways. It is by spending the time in learning new skills and perspectives that you find simpler, easier and less costly ways to make your business profitable, and in turn, serve your customer.

Train Your Brain!

Make it a
Buff Brain!

The Fifth Hour

WHEN TEAM BUILDING IS REQUIRED FOR PROGRESS

CHAPTER 6

THAT 5ᵀᴴ HOUR

If you are part of an MLM (multi-level marketing firm) or you run a business that requires you to work with a team of people as independent contractors, there is yet another hour to your week where you will be working ON your business, and that is Training Your Team.

For those of you with teams, we have to add an hour to our week because if these teams falter, it directly affects our business' bottom line (ex: training them to smile into a mirror when they answer the phone and stuff like that).

To give a bit of a recap about where we've been on this journey:

One hour a week is *Prospecting*.

One hour a week is *Following Up*.

One hour a week is *Connecting*.

One hour a week is *Training Yourself*.

Some of you will need to add an hour a week to Train the Teams you have working with your business.

Each week, the training I give my team is on the basics of the software programs we are using, how to serve our clients better and how to assist them in training the teams they themselves are running. Since my practice requires me to have teams of people working with me, there are times where it is important that I remind them of the greater vision of our work.

Remember your personal and professional vision? The life that you are trying to build for yourself?

This is where it comes in handy to articulate exactly why you are working the hours that you do and what you want from your teams. I also share with them in detail their personal importance and the part they play in that overall vision I have for myself and my community. Some people call this cheerleading. I call it keeping our vision crystal clear.

This step is usually forgotten (or never known) by folks who have worked for others most of their career. Now that you are working for yourself, this is required time that you spend to keep your brain from turning to mush and keep your teams in top performance for your business.

Training for yourself and your team is a form of connection that I have seen foster amazing "goodwill" that brought new resources and team members together that allowed my business to flourish. The harvest was years later, but a harvest there was to the tune of: $23,000 contracts, $31,000 contracts and $98,000 contracts. All because I took the time to train a contractor on systems I was using. That, in turn, caused this contractor to recommend my online university to a business owner who needed to train 112 of his employees. You see how that works.

The time you invest in others will eventually come around to you as dollars to keep your business in positive cash flow. Take the time to build this hour into your week. It will pay a handsome ROI.

Here are some points to consider as you train your team.

1. Be crystal clear on your vision for your company and your quality of life.

2. When Training Your Team, be sure they know your vision and are clear on how they fit into that construct. Repeat this in some way each time you meet.

3. Have them share their vision with you.

4. See how the two of you can harness the resources and people to help you move to your mutually beneficial goals and visions.

5. Always be present when speaking and listening to your team. Don't let your mind wander off when you're in the middle of their training session. Be fully with your team.

(Exceptions include but are not limited to: child tugging on your sleeve because the iPad won't connect to school event, smoke alarm is going off in the upper reaches of your apartment, or you hear a crash and "Uh-oh, Mom's gonna be mad when she gets off her meeting.")

Consistent Effort

CHAPTER 7

THRIVING AS A SOLOPRENEUR

M ost Solopreneurs love what they do. They thrive when they get to have the fun of working at their passion and making the world a better place one customer at a time. The thought of managing people, selling your business or making millions of dollars is not what motivates the modern Solopreneur.

The top three reasons for going into business for oneself are:

1. I want control of my schedule.
2. I need more flexibility in my life.
3. I want to be my own boss.

"Make More Money" didn't even make the top 20 list of reasons people become independent workers. We are seeing a massive trend in the business world that started quietly in the 80s and has been gaining steam ever since. Side-giggers, entrepreneurs and Solopreneurs are making up larger and larger sections of our nation's economy. Before COVID-19, the numbers of people that were going to become independent workers was expected to increase to 40 million in the USA by 2019. I think that number is way too small (especially after the workforce sees how much time and money they save working from home).

However, national trends aside, how do you personally thrive as a Solopreneur?

Setting a schedule for certain tasks allows you to move forward in your business doing what you love without the burnout associated with taking on more than your work-life balance allows. As your life changes and your family dynamic changes, you're able to ebb and flow with it by blocking time on your schedule. This is where you dedicate hours of your time to certain tasks that make your creative time a delight. It cuts down on decision fatigue and allows you to focus your creative talents during your high-energy and peak times. It is why most of my prospecting, follow-up and connecting time is done in the afternoon rather than early morning.

I'm writing my books, teaching classes and doing my high-energy projects in the morning hours and saving the phone calls, emails and scheduling appointments for my low-energy afternoons. When my creative juices are low, it is the perfect time for me to get on the phone doing customer acquisition, scheduling appointments and handling emails. Usually it is during my afternoons when my creative design skills plummet, so I spend it listening to clients, chatting with prospects and handling the details of running my business. My entire workday is set up and established in a way that is optimal for me to be at my creative best and keeps me in a positive, thriving state of mind.

My entire process is set up because I didn't ever want my business to "just survive." I wanted my business to become full-time. But it started as a part-time gig that I worked on when I wasn't teaching or during weekend hours when I was awake and my kids were still in their beds.

This process was coined in my head as my personal, Survive2Thrive Program. My brain likes to think in terms of processes and systems because of all the automation and robotics that I have done throughout my career. If I have a system in place for something, then I know that I will be successful in the outcome. No matter what it is. Why? Because even water can cut through rock given enough time. And as far as I am concerned, I always have time on my side. I'm patient. I'm willing to allow my ideas time to germinate, sprout and grow strong. I don't rush them along. When I truly took control of my calendar and started pacing my life according to my own design, that made all the difference.

Many people will try to prod and poke you into action. They may think that as a creative you are taking too much time, not progressing or that you are in fear. What I love about the systems I use is that people can implement them according to their own timeline, according to their pacing, and they don't need to rush and strain to reach some imagined goal of importance. Instead, they can move toward their dreams in a methodical, stepwise fashion that allows them to make progress every day without burning out from trying to do too much, too fast, against their better health and judgement.

It is all about that consistent effort. Tiny steps taken every single week. Take the time to make that consistent effort.

You have all the

TIME

you need
for none of us get
out of this Life alive.

Enjoy your
business & your life
– starting NOW!

CHAPTER 8

THE THREE BOX SYSTEM

During last year's training course, I was asked, "Janine, what do you do with business cards?" I hesitated, because I didn't know if the person was asking about mine, his or other people's. After a bit of questioning, finally it came out.

"Well, it's just that I have 5 shoe boxes filled with business cards in my home office, and I was wondering, what do you do with all those old business cards you've received from the networking events you've attended?"

My brain screeched to a halt. Wow. I've been in business for so long that I forgot some folks haven't set up a system on what to do with a business card that they find lying around in their office or home. Okay. Here you go, dear reader. This is The 3 Box

System that I use for old business cards that I stumble across as I clean up paperwork in my office.

Get yourself three boxes from the discount store. You know the $1-a-box kind that they use for kid's pencils? Looks something like this:

Label the boxes with the rather unimaginative titles of:

Box #1

Box #2

Box #3

Literally, those are the labels I have on mine. Then each time you find a business card on your desk, in a pile of papers, in a drawer or in a box of stuff on the floor of your office, place it into Box #1.

Now, if you are like my trainee mentioned above and you have 5 shoe boxes filled of old business cards with no memory of who the people are or where you got them, just fill up Box #1 so you can comfortably close the lid and work through those cards week by week until you've acted on each one of them. More on that later, first let me share the overall system with you.

Box #1 Business Cards (Prospecting)

1. Put all the old business cards you can find into Box #1. If you have more cards than the pencil box can hold, find a storage box (a shoebox is fine) to hold the rest of them. And until later, just fill up Box #1 making sure the lid can close.

2. Then, on the day and time you "Prospect" people for an hour, grab Box#1. Open it, grab a business card and call the number on the card asking for the person who is on that

card. What is the point of this phone call? To connect with the person who gave you that card, of course.

3. If you get voicemail, leave a message like this: "*Hey, Jane. I was cleaning out my desk today and I stumbled upon your business card. You know what is embarrassing? I can't even remember why I got it, but it was important to me at the time, otherwise, I wouldn't have made a point of keeping your card. Any chance we can schedule a phone call and catch up on your latest projects? Please give me a call back, and I hope to chat with you soon.*"

4. After leaving the voice message, text them on their cell phone and let them know you left them a message. Be sure to include your name in the text since they probably don't have you in their phone. I usually leave a text like this: "*Hi, Jane. Janine Bolon here. I left you a voice message. I look forward to chatting with you.*"

5. Then, I email Jane a quick message like this: "*Good afternoon, Jane. I just left you a message on your voicemail to let you know that I would like to reconnect. Please let me know your availability.*"

6. My favorite social media platform is LinkedIn. I go onto my account and search out Jane's name and make sure she and I are connected. If we aren't, I'll request a connection. If I don't find her on LinkedIn, I'll go to Facebook and ask to be her friend there.

7. I put Jane's name, phone number and other pertinent business information into my contact list and Master .csv spreadsheet and place her business card in Box #2.

8. I repeat steps 1–7 until my hour of prospecting is over and I move onto my next task for the day.

Pointers for Prospecting with Old Business Cards

- Throw away the card if you call the number and it is no longer a working number.

- Throw away the card if you call the number and your contact no longer works there.

- Throw away the card if the person you contact tells you that they are not interested in connecting with you (I've only had this happen once in 40 years!).

Box #2 Business Cards (Follow-Up Cards)

After you've spent an hour prospecting your old business cards, you will now have a group of cards in Box #2 where you are waiting to hear back from people to find out if they will schedule time for a call, or in my case, give me their address so I can send them a card.

What you do is wait 2 weeks before you attempt to contact them again. Do this calling during your hour of Follow-Up. Grab Box #2 cards and call all the folks you left messages for 2 weeks prior (that date will be in your Master .csv spreadsheet).

The activity is exactly the same with minor differences in the script. It looks like this:

1. Open Box #2, grab a card.

2. Call the phone number.

3. No answer? Leave a message: *"Hey, Jane. It's Janine Bolon, again. I left you a message about two weeks ago. I would enjoy being able to connect with you again. Any chance we can get on a phone call and catch up on your latest projects? Please give me a call back, and I hope to chat with you soon."*

4. After leaving the voice message, text them on their cell phone letting them know you left them a message. Be sure to include your name again in the text like this: *"Hi, Jane. Janine Bolon here. I left you a voice message again. I understand how busy life can be. I look forward to chatting with you."*

5. Then, I email Jane a quick message like this: *"Good Afternoon, Jane. I just left you a message on your voicemail. Let me know your availability over the next few weeks so that we can reconnect."*

6. I then put Jane's business card in Box #3.

7. I repeat steps 1–6 until my hour of Follow-Up is over.

Box #3 Business Cards (Connecting Cards)

After you've spent an hour prospecting your old business cards and an hour where you were doing Follow-up on the Box #2 cards, it is now time to take care of Box #3 cards. This is the point of no return for your contacts.

After you've waited two more weeks, Grab Box #3 cards and call all the folks you left messages for two weeks prior (that date will be in your Master .csv spreadsheet). You will be calling these contacts during your Connecting Hour. Go through all the cards where folks haven't gotten back to you with a time to connect via a phone call or given you any attention through email or Facebook Messenger.

The activity is exactly the same with minor differences in the script. It looks like this:

1. Open Box #3, grab a card.

2. Call the phone number.

3. No answer? Leave a message: *"Hey, Jane. It's Janine Bolon. I left you a message about two weeks ago. I would enjoy being able to connect with you again. Any chance we can get on a phone call and catch up on your latest projects? Please give me a call back, and I hope to chat with you soon."*

4. After leaving the voice message, text them on their cell phone again, and let them know about your message.

5. Then, I email Jane a quick message like this: *"Good Afternoon, Jane. I just left you a message on your voicemail. Let me know your availability over the next few weeks so that we can reconnect."*

6. I then put Jane's business card in the recycle bin.

7. If a contact has chosen not to respond to me with 9 messages left over a 6-week period, I don't follow through with them any longer.

8.   Repeat these steps until you run out of cards in Box #3.

Tips for Leaving Voice Messages

- Don't ever let exasperation, irritation or annoyance drip from your voice as you leave messages for your prospects—no matter how many times you've contacted a person.

- Smile into your mirror each time you get ready to contact the person whose business card you are holding.

- As you call each contact, act like you have all the time in the world to let them respond to you. Remember, we are prospecting here. It takes time to nurture these relationships. You are planting seeds. Seeds sprout on their own timeline, rarely ours. It is going to take time and patience before they sprout.

- If you feel like you are in a rush, stop. Breathe. Do some calming techniques, but don't ever prospect when you are feeling angry, frustrated, or cranky.

The 3 Box System grew out of my personal need to gain control over the paperwork flooding my workspace as my business expanded.

At networking events, I'd have 5–10 people handing me cards and asking me to follow up with them. It became obvious I wouldn't be able to keep track of all this paper online (at least for how my brain works). It calmed me down tremendously when I realized I could just move these cards from box, to box, to box as I let the weeks tick by.

At the end of each 6-week period, I am usually only tossing 2–3 cards. Usually I have reached someone on the phone or I got an email, Facebook request or LinkedIn connection from my efforts. I've had LinkedIn connections that were 7 years old contact me out of the blue using this system. You never know where your people will come from, but first, you've got to start the process by connecting with them.

 **#1 Prospecting**

 wait 2 weeks...

 **#2 Follow-Up**

 wait 2 weeks...

 **#3 Connecting**

 Recycle it!

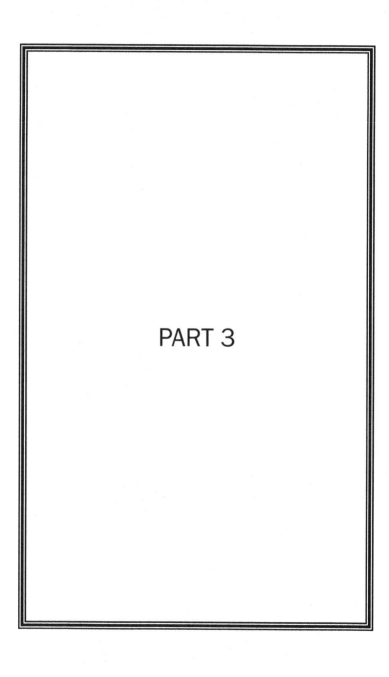

PART 3

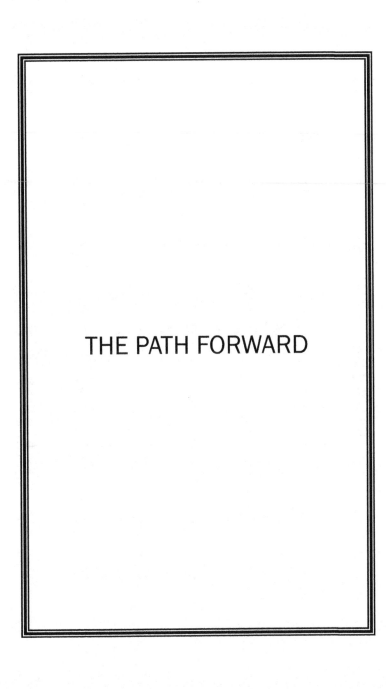

THE PATH FORWARD

Next Steps

CHAPTER 9

NEXT STEPS

I f you've arrived on this page after reading this entire book, thank you. And congratulations! I hope I have given you the necessary information required for you to rework your calendar so that you implement the required 4 hours a week to work ON your business.

Imagine what it is going to feel like to get up each day and know that you are continually in front of new people. You are consistently feeding your business with the prospects and leads that will keep your customer pipeline continually growing and flourishing without the complexity of many of the modern systems that require so much creativity on your part.

I hope that you are now convinced of the need for the 4-hour a week system that makes marketing and selling your business a breeze without the stress and anxiety that other systems can produce. I hope you've been inspired to think about the multiple ways you can reach out to your warm leads and bring them into your follow-up system with the intent of addressing their specific issues and how your business can solve them.

Ready to Get Started?

When you are ready to get started with any of my programs, the first step is a 15-minute Thrive Strategy Session with me so I can better understand your business and goals. Remember, every important and valuable journey starts with that first critical step.

Schedule a session with me today, and get started on the process of creating what I think is one of the smartest and most valuable marketing and business systems you can create, which is your very own 4-hour a week process for client attraction, retention and satisfaction.

My coaching programs and business systems are an investment and definitely not for everybody. But relative to the multitude of other ways you can invest your marketing dollars, my Survive2Thrive Programs are a bargain and give you a hugely valuable business asset that you can leverage for years to come.

I am a firm believer that you are uniquely qualified to be working with certain people. Not everybody will "get" you or what you and your business stand for. I know that's totally true in my business. In order for us to see if we are a good fit, I have a simple and easy way to further explore this opportunity, and it all starts with a 15-minute Survive2Thrive Strategy Session between you and me. This will give us a chance to "meet" and see if working together makes sense. To schedule this call, here's what to do:

1. Visit **JanineBolon.com**.

2. Review my videos, articles and programs.

3. Click the **ScheduleZoom** link and follow the prompts to schedule a chat.

This one-to-one call will help me understand what you do and what your goals are. This call is all about helping you decide if working together to get your Survive2Thrive schedule and systems in place is a good fit for both of us. It's a two-way interview to make sure we agree this is a good match.

I look forward to hearing from you, and more importantly, working together to turn you into a Thriving Solopreneur and help you create one of the most powerful client prospecting, retaining and satisfaction programs for your business: your very own *Survive2Thrive* process.

ABOUT JANINE BOLON

Janine is a testament to the power of perseverance. As an impoverished teenager in rural Missouri, she launched several successful businesses before putting herself through the University of Missouri biochemistry program by working three jobs at once and selling all her possessions. She can't remember a time when she didn't have some sort of side gig. Business was basically a hobby from her "real" job.

She worked for 15 years in academic and industrial research laboratories before spending the next 24 years raising a brood of four active spawn. In the past two decades, Janine has completed her M.A. in Education, homeschooled the herd, founded her Financial Literacy Firm (The8Gates), and written 9 books. And she teaches 15 online courses. When she's not teaching, she can be found sending cards to people she's just talked to or on the phone getting to know people like you. She has a soft spot for Solopreneurs.

A SMALL FAVOR

Thank you for reading *The Thriving Solopreneur*. I am positive if you follow what I've written, you will be on your way to having a more successful and thriving business!

I have a small, quick favor to ask. Would you mind taking a minute or two and leaving an honest review for this book on Amazon? Reviews are the BEST way to help others purchase this book, and I check all my reviews looking for helpful feedback. Visit:

JanineBolon.com/review

If you have any questions or if you would just like to tell me what you think about *The Thriving Solopreneur*, email me at: janine@the8gates.com.

ABOUT THE THRIVING
SOLOPRENEUR PODCAST

The Thriving Solopreneur Podcast is an interview-style program with host Janine Bolon and other Solopreneurs that started off with an idea that grew. We discuss the early days of launching their currently successful enterprise as well as focus on the basic principles and habits that got them where they are today. Thriving Solopreneurs are everywhere. They are serving their clients, customers and communities. They are leading by example and have wisdom to share that will serve your business challenges.

Each episode is focused on the business owner describing the challenges they had, the lessons they have learned, and eventually, the gifts of insight they were given about themselves and their communities. Even though you may never have heard of Janine's guests, you're sure to get several ideas and hard-earned nuggets of knowledge that are proven to work in the real world of online meetings, repeated phone calls and social media engagement.

Check it out on **JanineBolon.com** and if you think you'd make a suitable guest on the Thriving Solopreneur Podcast, visit: **JanineBolon.com/ guest** and connect with Janine.

Based on what I've read I will implement the following ideas for my business:

☐ _____

☐ _____

☐ _____

☐ _____

☐ _____

What day & time will I do my 4 Hrs a Week?

Prospecting

Follow-Up

Connecting

Train Myself

Team Training

What skills or books will I learn/read for my Training?

READER BONUS!

Your investment in this book entitles you to a very special gift that is the perfect companion to *The Thriving Solopreneur.*

This is a 7-part recording of an exclusive "live" training titled, **Your Critical 4 Hours a Week**, where attendees invested $226 to participate. And you can have it as my gift to you!

This training goes into greater detail on how to work Your Critical 4 Hours a Week "on" your business rather than "in" it. I describe the specifics of prospecting, follow-up, connection and the conversations I use along the way to move my prospects from warm leads into paying customers.

DOWNLOAD TODAY!

JanineBolon.com/readerbonus

Made in the USA
Monee, IL
04 May 2021